AF432293

BOOKS & SMITH
New York Editors

FLASH OF INSPIRATION

JACKSON PICHARDO

Translated from the Spanish by EDGAR SMITH.

A Books&Smith Indie publication.

To my father Ramón Pichardo,
for instilling in me the love of reading.

To my teacher Enrique Jiménez (Niño),
for setting in my soul the love of knowledge.

FLASH OF INSPIRATION

1.

Patience is the tree that bares
the best fruits.

2.

Laughing is the antidote to all
sorrows, an exercise of faith
in happiness that resurrects
from the bottom of tedium,
a statement of light
before the clouds of doubt.

Smiling is living
—A corpse's countenance is often too
serious.

3.

Time goes short and the hour approaches.
Hearts beat
and the moment implores
for the sound of yet another heartbeat,
of a heart that breaks,
like a wave,
the perfume of your kisses,

those...
dressed up as if for a grand ball,
like cherry trees
in spring,
adorned with chimeras,
flying furtively
leaving deliquescent trails
of recurring kisses
between one wait and the next.

4.

A life without difficulties
Or challenges to overcome
is like a meal without
flavor, color or salt.

5.

Nothing will prevent
love from manifesting:
—not the burning rays of envy
nor the freezing shadows of hatred.

6.

The night invites me to dream.
I want you to be there:
May your memory be my coat
Let it bring this delirium to rest.

7.

People say about more than one,
indolent on occasion
and swarming like flies over
fried entrails and pork rinds,
that they sold their soul to the devil
in exchange for a bottle of alcohol
and crawl like worms
to the beat of bachata and rum.

They are brothers of misfortune,
drunk at heart.
They hold hands
playing corruption
and proud they all go,
like sons of Ali Baba,
because,
even if the island sinks,
"nothing's going on!"

8.

I have no iota
of regret
for whom and what I have been.

I feel satisfied with my passage through
existence
because I have never spared any effort to
be myself and,
at the same time, bring the best of me
for the improvement of humanity.

9.

Life is Beautiful
when love is the balm
that soothes your pains,
when your dreams outweigh your
circumstances,
when your heart pounds, strong,
and reason is the hook
that strings your realities.

10.

The clock hands indicate
that time is passing.

We don't realize that,
in its wake, it drags
our essence
into the unfathomable abyss
we all sense
—but few want to accept
as something real.

Silence shades me and allows me to see
clearly
what my eyes find distorted by the filter of
emotions:

Countries with a short memory constantly
go astray
and lose their path.

11.

Let's go forward in the battle for life
—toward the conquest of our time,
with courage and temperance!

The world does not belong to the lazy
but to the brave who work on its
transformation.

12.

Every new day
brings us a new hope
wrapped in the silks of illusion.

13.

Life is more beautiful when we see it with
loving eyes, listen to it with patience, feel it
with tenderness, and digest it with
harmony.

14.

How long before the privilege of hospitals
stops being above the patients' right to
live?

An earthquake or any other natural event
can destroy

the building that houses a private clinic and
this will be rebuilt by their owners, but a
death due to medical negligence or
indolence cannot be restituted to a patient
or their family even if they are paid all the
money in the world.

15.

I'll wait for you
(under the light of the full moon
that illuminates the dark estuary)
with the calm of a seasoned voyager
who has traveled the seas of the entire
world
or the child who needs love and affection
with the firmness of a sailboat horn.

I love you.
At the precise moment I dress your dreams
with caresses and brief kisses,
the goblins and the breeze dance in
collusion:
How much I love you!
And the wind howls these words, too,
coming from the estuary
regardless of the storm, which drags on in
its sleeplessness.

I will wait for you and I love you,
No matter what the world says.
Your love is the highest peak and your
indifference
the deepest abyss.

I wait for you now, I love you.
Music for my infant soul,
tender and fantastic love
where my soul finds its rest.

16.

The sky is calm,
but its absence of clouds does not reflect
the voluptuousness of my soul.

17.

My ego was once a volcano.
Today, but a flame that progressively
fades away.

18.

The independence of a people is not a date
to be commemorated or celebrated in the
face of the past; it is knowing where you are
in the present and where you want to go in
the future, without depending on external
factors that change our aspirations.

19.

One of the great mistakes
of this civilization is that,
instead of looking for love,
people are looking for money;
and, living on illusions,
they die of disappointment.

20.

Gregorio Luperón,
Emeterio Betances:
Great lighthouses
in the Antillean firmament.

21.

The afternoon is scalding hot
and inspiration burns
my thoughts.

If I am not the sun in your sky, I will be
the silence that comforts your vigil.

Dwelling close to your lips rivals reaching
the gates of heaven.

22.

It is foolish of some people to expect
from life those things they themselves
are not willing to give.

They who cannot give do not deserve to
receive.

23.

If there is something wonderful about an
early morning,
it is being able to feel the quietness of
existence

and, in the middle of it,
the song of the earth
that, with its melody, opens the door
(from imagination) to other worlds.

In addition, it renews us
the opportunity to see
the magical dawn of a new day.
24.

Patience to walk,
consciousness to arrive
to our destination.

Life is a book only completed
with our last breath.

25.

The solitary thinker would like
to find the consolation
of a single idea that may emanate
from the flattering mobs of easy triumph.

In a wild society, which only worships the
strength and muscle of money, ideas are
diluted like riverbeds without vegetation.

26.

Evening falls
and a dim sun recedes
on the horizon in search
of rest for a new day.

At a distance, my thought
flies to forgotten places
from my childhood,

absorbing inspiration
from the honey color
a corner of the sky shares,
feeding on the nectar
of lavish memories
and warm kisses

How won't I evoke with melancholy
the twilight of this afternoon!

If *she* chisels the serenity of these words,
written under the sound of a bohemian
guitar.

The flowers of oblivion bloom majestically
on the cold wastes of time,

devoid of the fragrances of emotions,

while still projecting the colors of hope—
flashing, furtive,
in the heavens of the soul.

Oblivion is an unfathomable abyss
that swallows memories, an amnesiac
and subtle reminder of death.
(which advances silently to cover us
with its wings.)

Cursed absence, that swallows everything,
mysterious pit whose bottom never touches
the senses.

Every morning, I cut the red roses of
inspiration from my thoughts to place them
as an offering in front of the mirror of your
memory,

And, as a petitioner in expectation of the
miracle, I begin to pray an ancient prayer,
one of those that taste like a kiss and tense
with desire the beautiful Shulammite,
who awaits the consummation
of the miracle of the verb.

27.

I don't care about fame or money:
both are so ephemeral, it is enough for us
to close our eyes to lose them.

28.

I'm cold due to your absence,
but your memory illuminates my long wait.

I want to enjoy the nectar of your kisses,
the black light of your eyes, the warmth
of your hands,
the depth of your body.

There is nothing more exquisite
than a simple pleasure
on a poor man's palate.

29.

I know that many things will happen today:

The rays of the sun will go through my
window

and the smell of morning coffee will flood
my room, filling my senses with its aroma
of mystery.

I know that almost everyone outside will be
in a hurry fluttering like bees in search of
the pollen that will sustain life.

I know of many who will offer a smile
to the hammer that will come to bludgeon
their expectations of turning salt into flour,
mud into chocolate, and love into currency
to achieve dreams.

I know of some who will hide behind greed
to drink the honey produced by other
people's hands,
and will be proud of being parasites,
pretending it's a gift, not a burden
(which marks the victim and crosses
out the perpetrator).

I know of children who will not go to school,
who may eat but a single meal a day,
seasoned perhaps with lack of
understanding and attention,
minimally indispensable.

I know that life with its fast pace robs us

of the opportunity to connect with our
most intimate dreams and pushes us to live
off the feeling of hunger.

I know we are not a coincidence
nor an abortion of nature, because within
us the idea that we all have a purpose
does not stop beating: we must strive
to learn to be better, not be perfect,
but perfectible.

I know we are an intention and that we can
potentially be both flower and thorn.

I know we all know that,
above prejudices, we need each other.

The barriers between us are not natural
but pure artifice of social conventions.

I know that everyone can do their best
to materialize that old utopia: we are all
brothers.

Time offers no respite.
Sometimes it's light, sometimes shadow.

It goes with us everywhere but,
in the end, always abandons us.

30.

Pedro Mir and Miguel Hernández
visit me on this long night.

Their words are arrows for my ears
(asleep by force of routine), their images,
a captivity to hesitation and indecision,
their example, a lighthouse in the dark.

They invite me to dream
because I've been asleep long enough.

31.

Thinking is beautiful and unique
—and a single thought could be
interpreted in a thousand different ways.

The world, on the other hand, will spin
endlessly
yet always remain the same.

32.

What is left of the road traveled?

Maybe dust on the feet
and ashes in the soul—ashes as a result
of that corrupt flare that, like leprosy,
devoured The Republic,
turning it into a social mess, turning vice
into virtue
and virtue into sin.

33.

Crooked Politicians are the clearest
reflection
of a people who have lost their shame.

34.

The night arrived barefoot and silent.
It came through my window and, quietly,
whispered your name in my ear.
When I heard it, I felt the cold of distance,
the emptiness of oblivion.

35.

Life is a little fire already going out. I can
feel the cold breeze of memory murmur
an epitaph: it announces
the definitive winter when we will enter
the lenitive beaches of oblivion—The cruel
tomb of everything that's loved, the final
abode of truncated dreams.

36.

I dreamed of being a citizen of a people.
Reality condemned me to live together
in a jungle.

37.

Silence has its charm
when everyone talks and no one listens.

38.

More important than being a person of
words,
it is to be a person of deeds, because

the wind carries words away while deeds
have reliable roots in the soil of reality.

39.

Two lustful souls danced on the ballroom
of indifference; and that sad summer dance
ended in a French-kiss farewell.

40.

A gray cloud crossed the blue sky
on its way to infinity.

He left loaded with love, with experiences
dressed in beautiful memories,
with seamless honesty and Spartan
frankness.
God welcomes him in his sovereign glory.

Goodbye, old friend of the Hertzian waves;

You distinguished me with your friendship,
Oh fountainhead of humanity!

People like you are scarce today.

41.

I would like to sow the land of your dreams
with the seeds of my verb tonight.

And watch in the morning sun
how our dreams flourish in an
atmosphere of renewal.

The soul of the mob vibrates in the abject
peoples who, neglecting freedom, mentally
chain themselves to debauchery,
and, by avoiding duty,
renounce their rights, vegetating
like outcasts in their own land.

Goethe, who brought us the light
of his genius, with his shining words
still illuminates the dark
alleys of human thought.

How I would like to bathe in light
in a shower of stars.

Let's try to eliminate unnecessary haste
in our lives, because the reality
is that time does not pass, we pass.

Time is eternal and devours us

like Cronus did his children.

Time has always been the same—what
constantly changes is our awareness of it.

Let's live a quieter life—without laziness,
but calm.

People do not flourish under the perfume
of individual realities, but under
the fertilizer of collective dreams.

When a people stop dreaming,
they begin to disintegrate.

42.

You are the source that inspires my
thoughts, the body that contains them,
the volcano that ignites them.

43.

Hating is a way to debase ourselves
under the whip of ignoble passions.

44.

A kiss from you would be so powerful
that it would shake the world of my body.

45.

Afternoon of admonition and advent.

Evening thirst that precedes my thoughts.
Petrified childish laughter in my memory.

Outside, the zepphyr runs and dances
with its elements.

My soul rides on the wings of my memories.

Luminous thoughts come and go like
a southern breeze preceding winter.

The foliage of the verb covers everything
—leaving no room for weeds or mud.

My triumphant laughter over the steeds
of joy. My spirited soul does not demand
rest,
all it asks for is to rise to infinity
(without Icarus' weakness)

without
fear of falling into a pit.

Free as Ariel, sensitive as the noblest skin,
imposing as the look in the eyes
of the bison...

Just me, at the top of my thinking.

46.

Try to start the day with positive thinking
and the other steps will lead through
a more pleasant path.

47.

How I miss the crowing of the roosters
at dawn, that rural and countryside
symphony, which flaps its melodies
in my memory.

Sometimes I think that the greatest charm
of small towns is in the simple thing: their
people.

I must never get used to the rigid codes

of urban life,
of what we pompously call 'civilization',
if indifference is the morning greeting
on the bus and daring to share our joy
is a sign of madness.

The path of truth is not found
in doctrines or schools.
No teacher will ever show it to you.
You will only be able to find it and continue
looking for it in yourself, confronting
your experience of yesterday
with your experience today,
drinking from the source
of your own self.

48.

I only ask for the flower of your smile
and the light
of your black eyes, as a prelude
to a beautiful day
that the night will bring.

The afternoon comes alive to the rhythm
of the breeze and the caress of the sun.
Silence will be the cloak that covers us
From luminous envy and poisonous slander.

49.

Gratitude is a non-existent word
in the traitor's dictionary—where
the mirage of the terms forgiveness
and repentance abounds.

Don't waste your time miserably trying
to find an explanation for the motives
that guide a traitor's soul.

He usually carries the dagger under
the cassock and dwells under the shadow
of weakness, from where with religious
fervor he pounces against his prey,
with the sedative of forgiveness on his lips
and poisonous ingratitude in his fangs.

Don't be afraid of the atheist who walks
on a path without shadows and faces
the sun.

Fear the one who crouches behind
the shadow cast by a cross
—a dagger up his sleeve,
to ambush in the name of forgiveness.

50.

Sorayda,
sacred temple in the cult of my love.
Simple expression of beauty on the flower.
Calm water that crosses the rugged terrain
of my life.

Perfumed grass balm that comes
to heal my wound.
Faithful witness of the conjunction
between an exile's love and faith...

Your soft voice caresses the wounds
of a tormented heart, haven of fresh water
to quench the thirst of this old beast.
Proof of God's love for a waiting heart.
Unscathed hope in the middle of the storm.

Your kisses gave me strength
at that uncertain hour.
You transfigured my doubts into certainties,
cutting the weeds from my soul.
Bright star that today guides my spirit,
using the sweet melody in your voice,
today I offer you my life,
without hesitation or remorse,

Your love broke the chains of my suffering.

51.

(X-ray of a so-called patriot)

They love the flag and patriotic symbols
but collude to embezzle the treasury.

They defend the environment by word
of mouth, but, in the face of the sun,
are in favor of the mining that degrades it
—and of making this exploitation possible
at the hands of foreigners.

They defend sovereignty, especially against
the Haitians, but remain silent when
the interference comes from light-skinned
coastlines, weapons, and money.

They swear to fight for a national project,
but, as soon as they amass fortunes, send
their "savings" to "a safe place"
—like Miami, Switzerland or Panama.

The immigrant is attacked in the name
of "national origin," even if they have
a family member or friend without
immigration documents in other lands.

They are in favor of uprooting and violently
deporting the "Haitians who suck from
the breast that belongs to us," but are
unable to resist the temptation of fried
chicken, a bottle of rum, and $500 pesos
on election day.

They have two dreams that won't let them
sleep in peace: ousting the Haitians from
the homeland and getting a visa to live
in the United States or Europe.

They pay "onion" salaries to their
Dominican compatriots and "poison"
salaries to the unfortunate Haitians,
as a way to maintain progress.

Contrary to Duarte, they do not put their
money in favor of the cause of the republic,
but use the republic as an excuse
to increase their wealth.

52.

Whoever induces you to sow the seeds
of hatred will see you reap the fruits
of misfortune.

53.

Whoever truly loves, if they cannot build,
at least, will not destroy.

54.

Learn how to let go and you won't hang
on to anything.

55.

You will always be present at every step
I take, no matter what lights and shadows
walk with me.

You will come to me, perhaps without
knowing it, because memory lasts longer
than forgetfulness.

I will feel the caresses of your remembrance
like the heat of the sun reflected on a river
stone and experience a blush as your lips
touch mine.

I will live the bliss of the lamp that burns
while it shines with its beautiful fire:
product of the fuel of life.

56.

Before, our country was divided between
the PLD party followers and corrupt people.

Today, by whims of life,
our country is one and indivisible.

In the Dominican Republic, the music
of the official orchestra tells us that
everything is going well, but the lyrics
of reality tell us that we are a mess.

Who can I believe?

57.

I love Balzac's radiographic prose,
Verlaine's irreverence,
Victor Hugo's mental aristocracy,
and Rousseau's candidness...

but nothing comes close to the spirit

of a Parisian girl dancing to the sound
of a *Beaujolais*.

58.

We are all just drops of water.
Everyone seeks their destiny
in the incessant river.

59.

If you get paid with cynicism,
contempt ought to be the change
you give back.

60.

Afternoon of southern winds.

The sky is clouded with memories
that rush like kisses of dew onto the grass.

61.

We will dance in the rain,
celebrating the madness of our love.

Your voice will be background music,
your mouth,
an amphora of intoxicating liquor,
and the caresses of your hands,
the balm to cure my pain.

Tonight, I just want to count on
the complicity of your remembrance.

May memory touch my ears
with the echo of your childish voice;

from there, it lulls me tenderly and invites
me
to dream in the many paths to a verse.

62.

Do not expect from anyone
what you have given.

Everyone is different and it is inconsistent
with one's inner peace to give anything

with expectations of an exchange
—if what you give emanates from love.

Only the one who uses every breath
of their chest truly lives,
Every movement of their body,
Every sound of their thoughts,
Like a ladder that leads them
up to a purpose,
that takes them beyond the material
and on to the abstract.

Don't live in vain.

Try to do your best, spread love, sincerity,
peace, understanding, solidarity...

It doesn't matter if,
whoever you have in front of you,
is a miser.

63.

Only silence is fecund ground to fertilize
thought and have it give birth to
multicolored ideas
that fill life with realism.

64.

There are profuse and cold silences
—good to use as a slab to cover iniquities.

65.

Always give thanks upon discovering the
truth or perceiving the lie—life is made of
time that goes away and, in blindness, it
cannot be appreciated.

66.

Sometimes, the cynicism of the one
who hurts you is the best scalpel to remove
the mask of hypocrisy with which they
(slaves of opportunism)
wear their chameleon-like personality
—dirty player of simulation
and deception.

67.

I want to be as free as the wind
and not think

about where I come from
or worry
about where I'm going.

To live, only today is enough—
I free my soul from resentment
to let my chest breathe some love.

68.

I am just a bet on
the conquest of the intangible.

An intention that,
like a shining ray at night,

illuminates the pits of doubt.

69.

Beginning of the week,

riding on my dreams, guided by the illusion
of transforming harsh realities,
with the dawn star as a guide,
the world unfolds before my mortal eyes.

Always for love,
it's lovely and worthy to enter
the battle of life, unafraid of succumbing
to evil—with my heart held high
no matter how strong the storm.

70.

True freedom consists of breaking
the chains of ego
that bind you and destroying the jail
of illusions that imprisons you.

71.

Our dreams, goals and aspirations also have
their cycle: they are born, grow, often
reproduce and, finally, die.

Therefore, we must live them
with the same intensity and awareness
that we live in our biological body,
because the former is an extension
of the latter.

Because nothing is forever.

72.

Youth is a dream that vibrates and lives.

Old age is the dispossession of illusions,
the death of dreams.

73.

When I look at the Dominican social reality,
I prefer a thousand times the utopia of
believing
in its youth to living in the disappointment
of accepting that our elders failed us.

74.

Disappointment is an escape door
to desire that eats away your entrails.

It is also a ladder to other perspectives.

75.

Learning to fall is key to the warrior who
triumphs over adversity; and he stands on

an axis to shape his own will (without lights
to dazzle him or shadows to blind him).

76.

A thousand costumes deception has.

And a single truth, the naked soul.

That's why I loved you like this:
naked like a sunrise.

77.

The night is cold
and the Irish spirit takes hold of me.

In eternal movement,
like a breath of wind that kisses
the clouds and soars in search of freedom.

78.

The greatest works have been shaped
in an atmosphere of solitude. The rest
becomes noise: pure worldly routine.

Solitude is the perfect watchtower
that allows us to see
in peace the shadows of our weaknesses.
It is the strength of the spirit,
the bed on which our peace must rest.

79.

Oh Bacchus,

I am burned by the fever of Libya; bring me
dew from Frascati so that my soul rises over
the murderous dagger
—whose cold blade I can sense.

80.

Miguel Hernández: numen that flashes
in the dark night, portent of a new sun.

81.

Forehead held high and a haughty heart
when the storm gets worse.

82.

There is no path without obstacles
or horizon that may stop you once
you've chosen to venture forth.

83.

The afternoon sun illuminates an epitaph.

Only distance is agony,
only oblivion is death.

84.

No parasite is a friend of his victim.

85.

Abandon the life of those who
do not need your presence:
Exit through the door of understanding
and walk on the path of detachment.

86.

I don't mind losing
when there are victories that make you vile!

87.

When the night is over,
dreams awaken in green desire.

88.

Life goes by and the eras go by.

Steps go by and so do sorrows,

but hope never passes in a heart

that waits for tomorrow.

89.

When you offer your face and receive
someone else's back, it's synonymous
with your kindness and their blindness.

90.

As your days go by,
leave the luggage
with the things of life behind.

The soul is born naked and free.

It's also how it shall depart.

91.

They who know how to hold their head high
will not stop before irreverent contempt.

92.

Do not charge a bill to the wind
or storm that shakes
your body and troubles your soul.

In life, everything has a price to pay;
therefore, strive to be the captain
of your own boat in the raging sea.

93.

I miss everything
—except those who abandon me
for no reason.

94.

Life is the sum of living and letting go.

Enjoy the moment, bury the past and let go
of what doesn't want to accompany you
along the way.

95.

The soul bleeds when the chimeras break
and crystal tears expand among the stars.

96.

For Anthony Ríos

You went to take Charon's boat
to cross the Stygia lagoon.

Don't let your romance pass,
don't let your joy drown.

Farewell, sun of passions and misfortunes;
I remember you now and toast with what
you liked the most: a sip of rum...

To your memory, Bohemian.

97.

Conscience, more than a word,
is a moral imperative that calls us to action
in an era without role models,
where the cry for justice resounds
in the heavens and deaf humans march
towards the precipice of their own habits.

98.

In a society eaten away by the lumpen,
dignity becomes a degenerative tare
that isolates those who possess it
and perpetuates them in the ostracism
of the old and dark walls of mediocrity.

99.

Living in fantasy is the best way
to climb all the way to madness.

100.

Wrap yourself in silence and your soul
will not feel the cold of the vain word
that flows from the barren mouth.

101.

Time to sleep, time to return
on the paths of sleep
to the place from which we've come many
times without knowing what for.

Life is a light bulb that turns on and off until
its end, when it is turned off to the senses,
but lit up to eternity,

Because neither life nor death has age
—they are just expressions of our
consciousness.

Awake or asleep, it doesn't matter!

102.

Life is short as a sigh and deep as a kiss.

103.

Adulation to brute force and arrogance are twin sisters that inhabit mediocre minds.

104.

In the absence of arguments, the sword.

105.

The arguments of the sheep are the bread that the hungry mob of the circus feeds from.

106.

Glory is not a square where cowards dwell.

107.

If you sold yourself for a loaf of bread
and some fake coins, do not criminalize
those who defend your old ideas.

108.

In these moments of ideological uncertainty
(that affects many people), the important
thing is not to "have been," but, rather,
"to be," because the present is staggering
for the great majorities and the future
is an enigma to be unveiled.

109.

Don't let the tea of your dreams run out.

110.

The truth is the only wound
that leaves no scars.

111.

Don't try to free the mental slave who
kisses their chains. They could kill you
with that chain.

112.

Every friend we leave behind becomes
a star in the sky of our dreams.

How the wide sky is filled with
its resplendent lights,
illuminating with its memories
the already distant
and dark corners of our past!

A friend gone is a sweet,
unfinished melody that fails
to calm the melancholy
—a product of the emptiness
of his presence, of the cold of his absence.

A friend gone is a flower
that perfumes our soul in the loneliness
the path of life has in store for us.

A friend gone is a reminder that,

every nightfall,
we die just to be reborn.

A friend gone is an incomplete promise,
which strips us of the illusion of the
perpetual, and makes us face the brevity
of life—that everything flows away and
becomes past.

A friend gone is the hope that in other
places his warm presence can materialize
again and we can dance in dreams
to the music of new awakenings.

113.

The bootlicker and the flatterer go in favor
of the powerful or abusive, and always
turn against the victim.

114.

The traitor hates coherent people
because they are a slap in the face
of their resentment,
a sign of their moral inconsistency.

115.

Life is just a stop.

A single bead of an infinite rosary,
an intention that in the end fits,
completely, in a sigh.

Strive to live with love.

Try to avoid hurting without urgent need;
learn to let yourself go from everything.

Enjoy the simple pleasures without
complicating your existence, without
embittering the existence of others.

116.

Cold winter, cruel winter: impertinent
as a man, capricious as a woman.

117.

The cold winter, the cold death,
The hour goes slowly following its path,
leaving traces of boredom,

Ice flowers floating on the river;

And my thoughts, fragile ship
On its way to a port covered in fog
That agonizes in silence surrounded
by foam.

And my thoughts fly like hungry seagulls
after the sunlight that will mitigate the cold.

Meanwhile,
my hands cling to the helm of the boat.
Meanwhile, the spirits of the vines are
howling in the waters.

118.

I feel in my soul the cold
that drills your knees and,
in my heart, the blush of feeling
the warmth of your cheeks.

119.

Sketch my soul with your thoughts
and put wings on my illusion with
the depth of your kisses.

120.

Few in these times remember the worthy
man. Yet hardly ever will we remember
the sycophants and traitors.

121.

I have a homeland in every heart that beats
with dignity, in every conscience that is not
for sale.

122.

Who is more successful,
whoever has money to show
or their own identity and purpose in life?

123.

Everything is lost only
when you accept defeat.

124.

He who wants to harvest, sows.
Whoever doesn't do it is a fool
For they will depend on whoever sowed.

125.

No opinion is more intolerant
than that of the repentant fanatic
of any doctrine.

126.

I would infinitely rather die in solitude
and oblivion, defending the ideas
that I understand right,
than be remembered as a fugitive
or traitor to them.

127.

Ovando, Lope de Vega, Churchill, Ortega
y Gasset, Kennedy, Bolívar, San Martín,
Lincoln, Sarasota, George Washington,
Albert Thomas... these were surely great
personalities, but not as great as the
bootlicking of the Dominicans who made
the decision to name the main avenues
of our country after these names—when
there are plenty of Dominicans with more
than sufficient merits to be bestowed such
honor.

Oh, Guacanagaríx,
when will you let my people go free?!

128.

There are people who will not die
because their essence and deeds
transcend the barriers of oblivion.

Many others are dead in life: because
they live without knowing what they
live for.

129.

Flee from spiritual and moral destitution,
even more than from economic indigence,
because the latter may be temporary while
the other two are potentially permanent.

130.

Letter to Juan Pablo Duarte:

Today, once again, we are approaching the
day of your birth and, on this occasion, I feel
the need to write these lines to you, in order
to express what I see and feel as a Dominican
about the reality that the homeland is going
through (the homeland you dreamed of on
many nights and which you helped to build—
cause for much of your sleeplessness and
flame that, like leprosy, ate your life away.)

Many objective realities have changed since
that day, February 27, 1844; many are the
advances of our postmodern era, which
should allow your Dominican children to live
a different social reality from the one that
beats them today, but this has not been
possible, because Buenaventura Báez and

Pedro Santana's moral and political heirs have enthroned themselves in power to debase your work from up there.

I sense that, wherever you are, you feel lonely, and not precisely because you are not worthy to dwell in the hearts of your compatriots, but because selfishness is so great in so many hearts, that it does not allow many to follow your example of serving others.

I have read, as history is told, that you sacrificed your family fortune for the sake of independence; and today I see the politicians, who have misgoverned us, sacrifice the future of past, present, and coming generations to enrich them-selves at the expense of the people.

While your family's economic heritage diminished, as a result of their commitment to the cause of independence, the wealth of our rulers grows exponentially, since they are committed to theft, and it is they, with their bad example, who have overshadowed your legacy.

When young people hear your name mentioned on the lips of dishonest politicians, they do not pay much attention to the story of your example and sacrifice, because with such wicked messengers, their message about you is tainted by their actions.

On January 26, politicians will return to the public squares that bear your name and from there they will once again touch your story with their dirty hands, and in this way ensure that you are well dead in the hearts of the people, so that they can continue their feast of vultures and finish distributing the remains of the country.

But I have faith that, not too late, you will come again, in the visage of the people, to punish the corrupt who have abused and betrayed your example.

I know that you will not be petrified in the cement and granite squares where you are imprisoned today, that you will sprout in the neighborhoods and schools, and with a thunderous voice you will put the mark of infamy on the small fronts of traitors.

I will wait for that day, whether it is being a living person or inert ashes, because contrary to what they have sold us, you are not a saint and that makes it possible for the people to resurrect the greatness of your example.

131.

Between Kafka and Kundera,
and a succession of wandering images,
I ride my destiny.

132.

No matter how many difficulties life
brings before us if we have a big heart
for a shield and, for a spear, a sharp mind.

133.

Time runs over us
and we are invisible scars on its memory.

134.

When a country lowers their heads
to collect the crumbs thrown at them
by their rulers,
they end up feeding on ignominy.

135.

Contempt is the only currency
the ungrateful deserve as payment.

136.

It's raining.

The day mourns your absence.

The minutes pass quietly
over the empty streets of my heart.

137.

Like a comet, you passed over my life
Leaving a trail from a far-away light.

You gave me no time to reach you,
To abandon my bed dreams.
Where are you going?
I don't know,
Wandering star of my sky.

Passion knows nothing about decorum
Nor does indifference care about suffering.

They say 20 years is nothing; however,
I feel your absence at every step of the
clock, in the steaming pot of rice at noon,
in the complaint of a 'go and don't be late.'

How could I not remember you
between silly fights and healthy advice,
in the distance that points at us
from afar!

How if you were the brave Spartan,
who fought against life and its inexorable
circumstance—that, in turn, fought hard
to crush you.

20 years of absence and a memory
that dresses up to evoke your presence.

20 years without grandma,
20 years after the closure

of that school where we learned
that life is an ambush
and death just a mess,
which leaves us in ellipses....

This feeling of gratitude
that brands my bowels
with a mark of fire is still alive;

And, from afar,
the echo of a song comes to me,
and my heart shakes, as it evokes you
in my thoughts.

138.

Chants of a distant rosary come
to my ears on this cruel night
—that I feel like the Christ at his ordeal.

May the thorn of the rosebush
not become a dagger
that mutilates the image of your scapular.

Brutal hour that clogs my veins,
there is no counselor as cruel as sorrow.

Those who are born of existential boredom,

those do not remedy
the tortuous ailment
that corners a sore heart
in front of the cold stone
of a flowery temple of apostasy and evil.

139.

Living is to feel the vibration
of every second
in contact with our soul.

140.

I am only a thought that flies to the summit
of my dreams, where the stars shine in the
firmament of justice and love is the sap that
feeds each flower.

141.

Who am I?

Of your soul, a mirror,
and, of your vision, a telescope,
to contemplate your goodness.

142.

Blessed be the harvest,
the result of forbidden kisses.

143.

There is no greater pleasure for the spirit
than that of its body caressed by the soul
of wine.

144.

I'm walking, alone, through pathways
of mediocrity.

At the end of this,
life shines with the glowing sun of freedom.

145.

Fools love the continent.

The wise love its contents.

146.

He who lives on lamentations
stays in suffering.

147.

Out of all miseries, the one that debases
the human being the most is that of ideas,
because it turns them into a mirror of other
people's designs, because it turns them into
a toy in the hands of a reckless child.

148.

A life without a moral or spiritual purpose
is equivalent to a route without destiny.

149.

Choose living over being alive.

150.

Sometimes, silence walks slowly
on the path of oblivion
—and time is the only witness.

151.

Oblivion: the only cure for the pains
of memory.

152.

A definitive goodbye is equivalent
to a perpetual winter.

153.

Who understands the night and its whims?

Even more so when there is a thirst
for madness and a hunger for bodies.

154.

Pride is not a bright sun
but a random wildfire.

155.

When it's puppetry time,
no one cares about the strings
of the puppeteer.

156.

Living or vegetating:
the challenge of this multifaceted era.

157.

Love is the lightning that rips the veil
of the dark night, the wings of intention
on its way to conquer glory.

158.

The atmosphere of literature is the only one
that allows all forms of madness to breathe.

159.

For a teacher to remember one
of his thousands of students,
she or he must have been special
and pleasing to memory.
In order for a student to remember
a teacher,
his or her teachings must have left traces
in their life, have an attitude of gratitude
for what was received,
and maintain a long memory
when reaping the fruits
of the seeds the teacher sowed.

160.

Because we are only passing clouds
in the sky of eternity.

161.

Silence came in a hurry
and whispered your name in my ear.

162.

Your gaze is the balm that has healed
the wound of disappointment
on this forehead without faith.

163.

Dare to climb over the wall
of other people's opinion.

164.

The fire of inspiration burns my throat.

The thirst of your lips makes my soul
languish;

And you, indifferent,
pass in front of me with the arrogance
of the peacock.

Why did I drink from the fountain
of your evil to fall into the fatal precipice
of your body?

Why does it hurt me to drink
from your memory?

165.

Only by controlling the runaway horse
of your ego can you take the reins
of your own life.

166.

Your love was a lonely star
in the sky of my childhood dreams.

Your face was the sun
that illuminated so many dawns
full of fantasy.
Your lips were the fountain
of so many chimeras.

And the melancholy echo of your voice:
Prelude to my adolescence,
from which I sensed you.

167.

Of all the flowers I have found on the paths
of my life, none has left such a fragrance
like those that bloom in the fields of my
countryside, which could make my soul
open up to life in such a natural way
—like a sun-kiss on the face of the blue sky
to bewitch us with its tranquilizing
harmony.

168.

The afternoon begins to fall.
The night is lurking and my memory lights
up with the chandeliers of this rural
memory of my little town, which,
like a swallow,
flew away at the push of my people.

169.

I'm on my way to school.

I'm threshing a path.

It is sown with flowers

and their beautiful smells

bring me closer to you.

Like petals in the sky,

your black eyes shine,

kissing every footprint

I leave on the floor.

I'm walking on your memory;
My hands entangle in your black hair
like a nightingale's wings in the skies
of an estuary.

Where will your kisses lead me?

On this endless path,
in this ownerless land,
that one day shall see me leave.

170.

Willpower is the force
that moves the world.
Without it, life is a sterile pretext.

171.

The night vibrates like a poem.
It covers us with its shadow
and illuminates us with a full moon.

172.

We are simple footsteps
in the creation of the road.

173.

Those who are complicit in indignity
are unworthy.

174.

Never look for me on the side
of the indifferent.
My existence is a ray of light that tears
the veil of injustice, an expression
of humanity in continuous movement,
an intention of change about to materialize.

175.

The memory of you was born
out of my silence.

176.

A people addicted to spectacle and who,
at the same time, despise culture,
are condemned to live in the mud
of mediocrity and suffer moral darkness.

177.

It's early morning and the roosters
sing in my memory.

178.

Do not settle for what you have wielded
in your hands, but have the attitude
to march with readiness and serenity
to perfect your state of life. Slowly,
but with conscience and determination.

179.

Renouncing to fulfill one's duty
is renouncing life and the laws
that underpin it.

180.

One must have the courage and drive
to face the eventualities of life.
Because courage and drive are
the framework of our character and allow
us to stand over adversity.

181.

Loneliness is the only mirror
that allows you to see your true face.

182.

It does not matter if the world does
not agree with your ideas. It should
only matter that they do not negatively
affect others, but flourish in you.

183.

The one who has the most money
or knowledge does not live the longest.
The one who can constantly adapt
to the changes that occur in their
environment, unattached to their past,
and never dangerously moving away
from their present, does.

184.

Life is whatever you set your mind
to make of it.
You own the seeds of success
and failure.
You choose what you want to harvest.

185.

True freedom is not exclusively
a physical state, it goes further.
It is a mental condition carved
with conscience.

Therefore, the chains of ignorance oppress
the most yet are felt the least.

186.

To understand a truth,
it is not enough to open our eyes
to it, it is necessary to open our minds
to its true meaning.

187.

Not crying for what we have wanted
and lost is tantamount to filling every
space of our thoughts with nostalgia.

Each tear shed becomes a wing,
which raises, as it flies, our souls above
the sadness of the consummate, opening
with its random flight a new path through
which the sun slides.

Who hasn't cried for love?

Only they who have not lived and wander,
lost, in the twilight of their sleeplessness.

They who do not know the purity of a blue
sky and their own heart.

188.

Don't worry too much about
what others may think of you.

Focus on being you.

189.

Whoever exercises tolerance achieves
the strengthening of their soul.

190.

(Return to Septentrion)

My body still retains the aroma of coffee
from my ardent land that a poet once drew
on the same path of the sun.

There are still unaccounted beads
for the unfinished rosary of my affections,
which already faithless lips devoid
of illusion pray,
Seeing before their eyes how
civilization hits an inexorable setback
in the face of barbarism.

I still dream of not leaving the space where
every rooster's song is a prophetic message
to fertilize the earth with the seed of hope.

And suddenly I see myself alone, an eagle
that flies on a bald summit, in the midst
of a hellish storm of resolutions, emanating
from a thousand fallacious mouths, those
that dishonor the verb.

What can an outlaw of thought ask
of the Epicurean gods other than oblivion?

How to contain the sadness of seeing
the herd fall to the precipice while cheering
its executioners?

There is nothing to do on this dark night,
which covers the social conscience of my
country; Just let the dead bury their dead
and let the one-eyed men remain kings.

A country of one-eyed people that exalt
crime and degrade virtue to the swamp,
where the religious and the corrupt go hand
in hand, where being honest is an
unfortunate spectacle and being a thief
a role model.

I still love my land, no man's kingdom,
a surreal metaphor that evaporates into
an ocean of iniquities,

in the face of the complicit indifference
of modern Jeremiahs, who, in exchange
for a piece of old bread, decided to chain
the fate of their lineage with the chains
of vice.

When will Duarte come down
from the statues of the parks to walk
through the neighborhoods again?

I don't know.

In the end, history has to know.

Meanwhile, I hope:
"With the invincible hope
of those who've known defeat.[1]"

---

[1] A quote by Ruben Blades.

191.

What happened between us
carries little import.

Who was right is of little import.

At the time of our farewell.

I let you free to walk through life.

Leaving you free will heal the wounds
in my soul.

Let grudge not chain me to an illusion
already corroded!

I'll let you go free, like the wind,
on the edge of a hill.

May your memory never be like
the lemon burning on an open wound.

By freeing you from me,
my own life begins its liberation.
I leave you free, go in peace from
the vastness of the territory of my thought.

Giving you the freedom to leave,

the elixir to heal pain and suffering can
come to me.

I leave you free because freedom knows
no chains: it must never stagnate,
it must flow like the blood in our veins.

I'll let you go,
freeing myself from the yoke of judging you.

I am not God to condemn you
with absolute justice.

I'll let you free as it should be
So that your freedom will not be
my perdition.

I leave you free, wrapped in absolute peace,
may nothing chain us until eternity.

192.

How can I remember you in the midst of
your perpetual absence and refer to you
with respect if you were never there with
your presence, if your voice was never a
loving wind that taught me resilience?

You have already left without even the
mark of a kiss on me, regardless of my long
journey of care and suffering.

Curled up in your turbulent past, justifying
my sufferings, indifferent to my wounds...
to heal them, you didn't make any attempt.
You were selfishly *you*.

Today, I feel sorry for your surreptitious
and solitary departure, surrounded only
by strange hospitable hands.

May death give you the peace life never
could
and, from any pending grievance,
our souls, of one another, be free.

May the glory of God cover you
with his cloak in the face of the impossibility
of spraying your grave with my tears.

May my words not be heavy for your soul,
but a gale that drags with our karma.

A haven of peace, may your passage
be to paradise, contrary to your earthly life,
full of thunder, lightning and hail.

You are going to rest from that relentless
destiny.

From here, I say goodbye,
on the edge of my lonely path.

192.

Where did the seagulls go?

They flew on a pilgrimage with dream
leaving on their way, through my sky,
vapor of clouds of melancholy
and contemplation.

With them they flew,
like clouds to the north,
my teenage dreams of ephemeral
formation, abrupt and hot.

Like the clash
of clouds and their friction.

Lightning, hail, and thunder shone
on the vastness of my wide sky.

I, walking between hills and plains
and mountains, followed the trail
of those seagulls on the horizon.

Where do the seagulls
go with their acrobatic flight?

What is their challenge to sea,
land and sky?

What about my abstraction
when observing their flight?

To what remote place,
on their wings, did my dreams fly?

Birds of the sea, of heaven and daring,
carry between your gray-white wings
the spirit of my teenage dreams
and raise them to the infinite sky,
where the polar star shines

and, from below,

with the melody of the sea,
let us toast to its resurgence.

193.

Thank you, silence, for your kind company.

My body fills whole with the aroma
of your peace.

My soul rocks calmly sailing in your
emptiness; being you, silence, the best
liquor to intoxicate my boredom.

Before the vastness of your blurred form,
the reflection of my gaze moves slowly,

Scrutinizing in memory lost steps on already
gone roads...

No strength left for nostalgia,
screams or moans.

Only you, silence, fill the vast confines
of my soul with your mute poetry.
My quiet mouth, my still eyes and deaf ears,
are not a capitulation,
much less a hindrance;

My whole being is concentrated on you,

The one who comes to embrace me this
winter, bringing me absolute peace,
like the peace of the dead.

Freeing me momentarily
from the noise of life and its injustices.

194.

When love dies, there is a deep emptiness:
dark as night, intense as cold.

Shock to the soul: where there were flowers
and thorns, nothing is left.

When a great passion dies,
Your heart is no longer a garbage dump
of rubble, of vanities,
of them—who became your gravediggers.

The death of a great love
is the transformation of life.

It tells us there is no "the end"
behind a farewell;

Only a change of season
on the immense wheel of life.

Don't cry for the love that died
silently one morning.

No matter how much you loved
or if your lives were marked,
If this was your last pain
and you sensed the coming of dusk.

When a love dies, it resurrects life.

Longings return without
the pain of wounds.

The fresh breeze kisses your forehead
With new devotion.

And fortune is great in that reincarnation.

195.

To heal the wounds of the soul,
it is of the utmost importance to accept
the unappealable verdict of those things
that happen or happened,
which we cannot change.

Understand that we are only a leaf
on the tree of life, made up of multiple
seasons, an invitation not to cling
to either good or bad things,
to learn to flow according
to the circumstances of time.

Desist from judging the attitudes
and behaviors of others towards us,
no matter how much we understand we
deserve recognition or esteem from them.

Delve into your essence, in search for
the answers about who we are, what our
purpose is and how to walk the path of its
realization.

Prevent the ego from overflowing the dams
of goodness, compassion and love, which
underlies you, turning you into a toy of low
passions, a weather vane moved
by the wind of other people's opinion.

Love yourself, without the narcissistic
clothing of vanity, that eats away at
everything, of the presumption that alters
everything, and of the ego that hurts
everything.

196.

Alone, I walk through valleys of silence.
At a slow pace and with a distant look,
sailing in absentia.

Lost steps in the labyrinth of time.
Absence of desires, nullity of fire,
illusion in decline.

My soul rocks quietly between
the zigzagging steps.
I journey without haste or emotion,
letting myself be carried away
by the path like dead leaves pushed
by the gale of destiny.

Undaunted by sporadic songs
born of wild throats,
I go with myself, at the center
of the universe,
full of emptiness Like the wide sky,
insensitive to pain, to love and illusion,

Carcass of memory,
shipwrecked in nothingness,
Point of departure and final arrival,
in the form of dawn.

It's just me: the essence of nothing.

Soft breath suspended in the ether.

No desire to fall like dew on the plain,
without struggling to stay in the estuary.

Just aspiring to be finally forgotten.

We are nothingness transmuted
into oblivion.

Eternal coming and returning
of the same paths.

Jackson Pichardo was born in June 1973, in the city of Moca, Dominican Republic.

From a young age, he showed concerns about social causes and became an activist in student movements, sports and cultural clubs.

He had an ephemeral militancy in the Dominican Liberation Party between 1993 and 1997. In 1995, he enrolled in the faculty

of legal sciences of the UASD university   ,
in pursuit of a Law degree, but he had to
interrupt this in 1997 when he moved to the
USA, to reside in New York City. Between
2006 and 2011, he was involved in
humanitarian work, being part of the board
of directors of the Dominican Health
Organization, ODOSALUD.

At the same time, he wrote an opinion
column on topics of contemporary political
and social affairs, which was published as a
guest column with some frequency in media
, such as Diario La Prensa in New York City,
and in several Online media outlets in the
Dominican Republic and Latin America.

Since 2010, he has worked for the consulting
company Muñoz y asociados, where he has
participated in different projects with a local
impact in the state of New York, as well as in
the Dominican Republic.

This is his first literary publication.

Other books by Books&Smith Indie:

MY CHILDHOOD MEMORIES
Belkis M. Mars

THROUGH THIS STRANGE WINDOW
Edgar Smith

BROKEN CRYSTALS
Pedro Santana

VIENTO DEL ESTE / WIND FROM THE EAST
Luis Navarro

FIPTISIO '89
Elssie Cano

www.booksandsmith.com
booksandsmith@hotmail.com

Dear readers, thank you for your time. As you may have noticed, the quotes and poems in this book do not have titles; therefore, we have not added an index, as you may be accustomed to. We hope you have enjoyed this work.